THE STIGMATA
AND
MODERN SCIENCE

By

Rev. Charles M. Carty
RADIO REPLIES PRESS, ST. PAUL, MINN.

TAN Books
Charlotte, North Carolina

Nihil Obstat: Gualterus H. Peters, S. T. L., Ph. D.
Censor Librorum

Imprimatur: Gulielmus O. Brady, D. D., S. T. D.
Archiepiscopus Sancti Pauli
Paulopoli, die 24a Aprilii, 1958.

The NIHIL OBSTAT and the IMPRIMATUR indicate only that this manuscript has been read before publication by one who is competent; that in the manuscript he has found nothing contrary to the faith of the Catholic Church nor to its moral teachings. In indicating that nothing such has been found, there is no implication that those who grant the NIHIL OBSTAT or the IMPRIMATUR agree with the contents, opinions or statements expressed in the manuscript.

Originally published by Fathers Rumble and Carty, Radio Replies Press, Inc., St. Paul, Minn., U.S.A.

Complete and Unabridged

ISBN: 978-0-89555-104-7

Printed and bound in India

TAN Books
Charlotte, North Carolina
www.TANBooks.com

2013

The Stigmata and Modern Science

The following definition of Stigmatization given by Fr. Pfulff, S.J., in *Kirchenlexicon* may be said to represent the mind of the Church and the sentiment of the faithful with regard to the stigmata:

"Stigmatization consists in participation in the Passion of Christ in a way that is shown outwardly by marks on those parts of the body where Christ bore His wounds. It is a charisma or supernatural gift."

The external marks of the wounds of Christ are then only the material element of Stigmatization; to be regarded as stigmata in the ecclesiastical sense they must be accompanied by a participation in the sufferings of Christ. And not all marks or wounds, even if they be on those places where Christ bore His wounds, are regarded as even the material element of Stigmatization. To be regarded as stigmata in the ecclesiastical as against the medical meaning of the term, these wounds must not be mere surface marks such as are sometimes produced by hypnotism, but must be deep wounds such as, for example, those of St. Francis of Assisi; they must not vanish after a short time but must remain fresh for years without suppurating, and when they bleed they must emit fresh blood. In addition, these wounds which form the material element of Stigmatization must be accompanied by a participation in the physical sufferings of Christ's Passion and by the profession and pious practice of the true Faith in the Catholic Church, before they can be regarded as stigmata in the strict sense.

The vocation of the stigmatists is to suffer a share of the Passion of Christ—which exceeds all earthly sufferings. St. Margaret Mary Alocoque participated in the agony of Christ in the Garden and felt that death itself could hold nothing so painful for her. What must it be then to share in all the sufferings of the Passion, including the crucifixion, as most of the stigmatists are asked to do? Need we wonder then if Almighty God allows the stigmatists to get a glimpse of Thabor occasionally? Need we wonder if He gives them special gifts? St. Paul says: "we are the sons of God . . . and joint heirs of Christ, yet so, if we suffer with Him, that we may also be glorified with Him." (*Rom.* 8:16-17).

In the history of the stigmatists, we find that the stigmata were always accompanied with other charismata such as living for years without earthly food, the gift of prophecy, the gift of reading the secrets of the heart, the faculty of distinguishing between sacred and profane objects, the gift of perceiving the presence of the Blessed Sacrament in places hidden from view.* In our own day all these charismata are found united in the person of Teresa Neumann. These various charismata that accompany Stigmatization mutually support each other and help to prove that the stigmata are genuine. Conversely, if any fault against faith or morals is detected in the stigmatists by proper authority—the Bishop or the Holy See—it is a sign that the person in question is not corresponding to the graces that go with the stigmata, or that the stigmata were not genuine. But as long as the proper authority issues no condemnation, the faithful need not be disturbed by shrill warnings from unauthorized individuals. In the long list of the stigmatists since St. Francis of Assisi—which Dr. Imbert Gourbeyre puts at 321 up to his

* See Pfulff. *Kirchenlexicon.* VIII.

time—only a few of those who had real external marks of the Wounds of Christ were found to be unfaithful. A few Catholic writers who hold peculiar views about the stigmata refer to the few cases of lapse with apparent triumph, as if they proved that the possession of the marks of the Wounds of Christ was of no consequence. The extraordinarily high proportion of stigmatists faithful to their glorious but painful vocation, amounting to nearly a hundred per cent, may be attributed to the fact that, in the Providence of God, only those receive the stigmata who have been tried in the crucible of suffering for many years and who have been found faithful.

On this subject I take the following quotation from Mystical Phenomena by Archbishop Teodorowicz:

"Because the stigmata make the most difficult demands on the soul, on its ability and willingness to suffer in its mystical life, these souls must undergo long trials and sufferings. Only after a period of purgation in the glowing flame of pain do the wounds begin to make their appearance . . . Before they themselves appear, they prepare the body by means of manifold suffering, as though it were necessary to cultivate and harden it for continuous suffering. The bestowal of the stigmata is always preceded by corporeal sufferings; and the soul, thus cleansed by pain, is attuned to higher things and trained to valiant courage. . . .

"Practically the same process takes place in all the stigmatists; first severe illness or great interior commotion, then the appearance of one or other wound, rarely all of them together. . . .

"Thus a long illness preceded Teresa Neumann's Stigmatization. . . . In the measure that the painful sufferings increased and continued, her soul through the mysterious operation of grace became more perfect. The great difference between the condition of her soul at the beginning of her sickness and at the climax of her painful sufferings can be almost perceptibly measured. In the beginning we notice an actual yearning for an active life, against the visitation of the cross. At the end, however, we notice that she dies to all that is not God's will and is completely resigned to the divine guidance."*

The case of St. Francis of Assisi cannot be regarded as an exception to this rule. It is true that his vocation was to represent the poverty rather than the Passion of Christ, and to perpetuate the idea in a great Religious Order; but when his first mission was fulfilled, he was chosen for the second one, to bear in his body the marks of the glorious wounds of Christ.

The object of Our Divine Lord in granting the stigmata to St. Francis of Assisi and the lesson the faithful are expected to draw from them are expressed in the collect of the Mass for the Impression of the Stigmata of St. Francis. The words of this prayer can be applied to all the stigmatists who came after him:

"O Lord Jesus Christ, who when the world was growing cold, in order that our hearts might burn anew with the fire of Thy Love, didst in the flesh of the most blessed Francis renew the marks of Thy Passion; mercifully grant by his merits and prayers that we may carry our cross and bring forth fruits worthy of penance."

Some few Catholic writers make St. Francis the criterion by which the genuineness of the other stigmatists is to be judged. Before receiving the stigmata a person should, according to these writers, have arrived at the heights of mystic contemplation, and the conferring of the stigmata

* Archbishop Teodorowicz, pp. 279-280.

should take place while the recipient is in ecstasy of love. No one can lay down rules for the Almighty, nor can we get an idea of His designs from a single instance such as St. Francis of Assisi; particularly when his chief vocation in life was not that connected with the stigmata. If we were to seek the meritorious cause of the favor in the case of St. Francis, we should rather find it in his great compassion for the sufferings of the Saviour combined with his own great sufferings than in seraphic love. As we shall see in greater detail later on, the external marks of the wounds of Christ on Teresa Neumann correspond exactly to those on the hands and feet of St. Francis of Assisi.

There are many books giving lists of the stigmatists all of whom have lived since the time of St. Francis of Assisi but the only attempt at a complete list is made by Dr. Imbert-Gourbeyre, a Paris doctor, who published two volumes on the stigmatists at Paris in 1894. In Dr. Imbert-Gourbeyre's list are included all those who can lay claim to the title, including those who bore the stigmata invisibly, such as St. Margaret Mary Alocoque, who had an invisible crown of thorns. Out of the list of 321 stigmatists which he gives—of whom 41 were men—62 have been either canonized or beatified, and the causes of many others have been introduced. This is a very high percentage amounting to one in five, and there is a strong presumption that the others, with the exception of a few who did not persevere, were very holy persons. The percentage of canonized among religious does not amount to one in ten thousand.

Out of this list of 321 stigmatists (which some think should be 400 if all who have a claim are included) there are four test cases which have completely defeated the efforts of those critics who argue that natural causes are sufficient to explain Stigmatization. Qualified opinion now regards those four cases as miraculous. They are the cases of St. Francis of Assisi and Teresa Neumann, whose stigmata have the form of fleshy nails; and of St. Mary Francis of the Five Wounds and Padre Pio, whose stigmata have the form of fissures penetrating the hands and feet like those in Our Lord's hands and feet when He was taken down from the cross.

St. Francis of Assisi received the stigmata in September 1224, two years before his death. An account describing his stigmata, written by Thomas de Celano four years after the death of the Saint, has come down to us. According to that account, the stigmata of St. Francis were not in the form of wounds made by the nails, but of the nails themselves; and in the Bull of Alexander IV (1255) it is stated: "In his hands and feet, St. Francis had most certainly nails, well formed, of his own flesh or of a substance newly produced." St. Bonaventure adds that he was informed by people who had seen the stigmata that the heads of those nails in his hands and feet were round and that the points were bent like nails that had been clinched. The points of the nails in the feet projected so far that a person's finger could be inserted under the bend. In an early picture of St. Francis, now at Pescia, which represents the stigmata on the hands, the head of the nail is shown on the back of the hand and the point, which is turned down as if clinched, is in the palm. Fr. Herbert Thurston, S.J., who had read through Dr. Imbert-Gourbeyre's two volumes and was satisfied that there were at least fifty or sixty well-attested examples of visible stigmata, stated; "In no one, as far as I am aware, of the fifty or sixty well-attested examples of visible stigmata which have been recorded during the past seven centuries, is anything to be met with which can be put in comparison with these rigid protruding nails." Fr. Thurston admits that it is in the power of God to produce such a marvel, but he adds, "Very exceptional evidence would be required before a miracle so unexampled in all recorded history could expect to gain credence"; and he continues:

"The marvel described in St. Bonaventure's *Legenda Minor* and in the *Fioretti* is almost startling, and it seems to me that there is much excuse for those who find it easier to explain away the language of Bonaventure and even of Celano than to accept these statements at their face value."

And a few pages later, Fr. Thurston states:

"No power of auto-suggestion, no abnormal pathological conditions, could enable a contemplative to evoke from the flesh of his hands and feet four horny excrescences in the form of nails piercing his extremities and clinched at the back. Such a manifestation, if it occurs, must surely be held miraculous. The question, however, is whether the evidence allows us to affirm the existence of these excrescences."

If Fr. Thurston had gone to Konnersreuth, he would have had his doubt settled, for the stigmata on the hands and feet of Teresa Neumann correspond almost exactly to the account of the stigmata of St. Francis given by Celano and St. Bonaventure. As we have in our own time in the person of Teresa Neumann a case of those horny excrescences piercing the hands and feet and clinched at the back which Fr. Thurston regards as evidently miraculous, it is fair to assume that the description of Celano and St. Bonaventure must be taken literally. The extraordinary form of Teresa Neumann's stigmata has been verified by representatives of the Holy See and photographs have been taken.

Dr. Louis of Versailles visited Konnersreuth in 1930 and examined the stigmata on the hands. The following is how he describes the marks in the left hand in his booklet entitled, "Holy Week at Konnersreuth":

"On the back of the left hand I see a head of a nail, rectangular in form, slightly longer than wide in the direction of the hand. The rectangle which it forms is admirably regular and has its edges delicately adorned with zig-zag borders. It is about 15mm. by 10mm. These borders are slender and sharp like the edges of a nail forged with a hammer. The head of the nail itself is slightly arched and is round like a dome. The top of the dome itself is about two or three millimeters in thickness. It shows flat marks in several places resembling those produced by a blacksmith's hammer on a piece of iron. The color is reddish brown like a seal of ancient wax.

"I now examine the point of the nail on the palm of the left hand. It is lying on the skin in the hollow of the hand, turned obliquely down as if by a hammer, with the point turned towards the outside of the hand. It emerges, thus bent, for a length of about 15mm. It adheres completely to the skin. It is about 4mm. in thickness and is rough and round in form. It is of the same brownish colour as the head of the nail but the cicatrice border around it is not so well defined."

This description was written in 1930. A similar description is given by F. X. Huber in his book published in 1950, with the addition that these nails were hornlike formation and that they pierced the hands and feet.

This description by Dr. Louis, shows that the stigmata of Teresa Neumann resemble very closely those of St. Francis of Assisi as described by Celano and St. Bonaventure. Fr. Thurston quotes Catholic writers who think that the description of the stigmata of St. Francis is exaggerated and he inclines to that opinion himself. We therefore give further quotation from F. X. Huber's book which corroborates the description given by Dr. Louis and show that Teresa

Neumann's stigmata are really horny substances in the form of nails piercing her hands and feet—a form of stigmata for which no natural explanation has even been attempted.

"The stigmata formed gradually; first on the backs of the hands, then in the palms; they were at first open, then the wounds became covered by a scab and surrounded by scarring. But these wounds do not bleed outside the Passion ecstasies; neither do they moisten nor discharge; outside the Friday ecstasies they are absolutely dry. They are new growths, hard and horny, around which lies an elastic, delicate membrane which breaks and bleeds during the Passion ecstasy and at the end of it closes again. (cf. Lama, Yearbook, 11-17).

"Inside, on the palm, the marks are narrower and longer. The wounds are exactly alike—something that certainly would not be so if anyone had tried to make them himself.

"The fact is to be emphasized that the wounds on the hands did not first appear where they might be expected to appear—on the palms of her hands—and so for this and many other reasons auto-suggestion as an explanation must be ruled out. They started on the backs of the hands—only later did the marks work through to the palms.

"When the stigmata do not bleed, they are covered by a fine membrane and appear sometimes a deep, dark red, sometimes fresh ruby red. According to independent medical evidence they are genuine if they arise without any artificial interference and are obtained without the taking of any action . . .

Dr. Witz noted in 1931:

"On the back of the hands stigmata 9-11mm. wide; in tablet-like relief raised above the surrounding skin about 2-2.5mm., on all sides alike steeply falling edges; surface fiat, but glistening."

"In the Yearbook for 1931, Ritter von Lama again gives the result of several investigations of the changes in the wounds observed at that time. These lay essentially in the fact that a sort of nail forms in the wounds and seems to consist of firm, grisly flesh; one got the impression of a forged iron nail which goes through the hand from outside to the inside, the end of which appears to have been bent round by a hammerblow. Between the crust in the middle of the wound and the normal skin lies a brighter edge, grooved and delicate; and through this edge or membrane the wounds bleed. The wounds cause very little pain, only when Teresa Neumann extends her fingers, the stretching of the skin does hurt a little.

"Dr. Babor noticed the sudden outflow from the right shoulder of fresh, cherry-red blood in 1932 during the vision of the clothes being torn from Christ before the crucifixion, and in 1934 at the fifth Station (where Simon of Cyrene had to help Our Lord carry the cross) when the cross was thrust on to Our Lord's shoulder by Simon and he adds:

"'As a proof of the miraculous nature of these phenomena, nothing can be more convincing to a doctor than the remarkable way in which the times that Teresa Neumann's stigmata bleed correspond with the times of Our Divine Lord's sufferings. Thus, her hands bleed when our Lord's hands are bound in the Garden of Gethsemani, the stigmata of the scourges bleed at 6 a.m. (8 a.m. Jerusalem time) when Our Lord was scourged; the bleeding of the wounds on her head begins soon after as she sees the Crown of Thorns placed on Our Lord's head; the shoulder wound bleeds during the vision of the carrying of the cross and again when Our Lord is stripped of His garments; and the wounds of her hands and feet bleed profusely during the vision of the crucifixion.'

"Teresa Neumann often submitted to medical examination of the heart wound—at the desire of, or with the approval of the Church—this was measured, touched, irradiated, X-rayed, described; was still oftener observed when active and bleeding; then, too, when Teresa Neumann was in her Passion ecstasy, knowing nothing of what was going on around her or what was done to her, when the wound bled without her knowing, when her natural consciousness, her ordinary attention to physical happenings, when any influence by her on the process of bleeding, were completely eliminated.

"This nail-shaped formation of the wounds (occurring in past centuries in the case of some stigmatists), was something that Teresa Neumann soon noticed; when the progressive consolidation of the formation, it gave her the feeling as if something were pricking in the stigmata.'

"Outside the period of the Passion ecstasy these formations feel hard, almost horny; and yet are most sensitive; just at the beginning of the Passion ecstasy from Thursday evening on, they become soft and super-sensitive like fresh wounds."

While the stigmata of the hands and feet of St. Francis of Assisi and of Teresa Neumann are almost identically alike and are in the form of fleshy nails that pierce the hands and the feet, those of Saint Francesca delle Cinque Piage of the 18th century and of Fr. Pio of our own time are also alike and are of the opposite kind to those of St. Francis and Teresa Neumann, being empty wounds through the hands and feet, like the wounds on Our Divine Lord's body when He was taken down from the cross. Of the wounds of Maria Francesca, Don Paschal Nitti, one of her confessors, gave the following testimony on oath at the process of beatification:

"I have seen them, I have touched them, and to say the

truth I, as the Apostle Thomas did, have put my finger into the wounds of her hands and I have seen that the hole extended right through, for, in inserting my first finger into the wound, it met the thumb which I held underneath on the other side of the hand."

With regard to the stigmata of Father Pio, we read in *A City on a Mountain* by Pascal P. Parente:

"The Provincial Superior examined the wounds immediately after their appearance and said that, looking through the wounds in the palms of Padre Pia's hands, one would have been able to see in all its details a piece of writing or another object placed on the opposite side of his hands. . . . The wounds in the feet show the same characteristics. . . . The wound in his side is about two and three-quarter inches long and has the shape of an inverted cross, such as a cut by a lance would have caused. These wounds have persisted unchanged now for thirty-five years."

After a year and three months of frequent tests and examinations during his five visits to Padre Pio, Dr. Romanelli wrote the following report:

"The wounds which Padre Pio has on his hands are covered with a thin membrane of reddish colour; this is not tinged with blood. I am convinced and am quite certain that these wounds are not superficial. By pressing them with my fingers, I have felt a void that goes through the whole thickness of the hand.

"I have been able to ascertain that if I pressed them more strongly my fingers would meet. An experiment of this kind, and in fact, pressure of any kind, causes the Father intense pain.

"However, I have submitted him to this painful experience several times morning and night, and I am bound to admit that each time I arrived at the same conclusion."

"The lesions an the feet present the same characteristics as those of the hands but on account of the thickness of the feet I have not been able to make the same experiment as with the hands (i.e. to make my fingers meet in the middle of the wound).

"The wound of the side is a clear cut parallel to the ribs, seven to eight centimeters long, but of a depth difficult to ascertain. It bleeds abundantly. This blood has all the characteristics of arterial blood, and the edges of the wound show that it is not superficial.

"The tissues that surround the lesion show no inflammatory tendency but are painful to the least touch. I have visited Padre Pio five times in fifteen months, and though I have observed some modifications I have not been able to find a clinical formula to classify these wounds."

Leaving aside the cases of St. Francis of Assisi and of Saint Maria Francesca, which are undoubtedly miraculous, Fr. Thurston declares with regard to less remarkable cases:

"Whatever such investigators as Bourru, Burot, Charcot, Bourneville have succeeded in producing by suggestion in their hysterical patients, falls very far short of what is recorded of St. Gemma Galgani, Domenica Lazzari and a dozen more whose manifestation cannot here be described."

St. Gemma Galgani cannot be reckoned among the stigmatists in the strict sense, for, although her wounds were very real when they appeared once a week, they were not permanent; however, Fr. Thurston includes her on his list of true stigmatists. The case of Louise Lateau, the Belgian stigmatist, (1850-1883) is different. She received the stigmata in 1868 and they continued until her death.* Like Teresa Neumann, she lived on the Blessed Sacrament alone from

* Cfr. The Two Stigmatists by Fr. Carty. pp. 125-130.

the time she received the stigmata. Doubts about her case were cleared up before her death. The Royal Medical Academy of Brussels sent two doctors, Dr. Warlmont, a Catholic, and Dr. Crocqu, a Freemason, to carry out an investigation. The following statement was signed by these two doctors after the investigation: "The stigmata of Louise Latent' are a fact and free from deception. Medical science can give no satisfactory explanation of these phenomena."

This statement of the two Belgian doctors might be applied to all the stigmatists who had the permanent marks of the wounds of Our Lord, shared in His sufferings and lived a holy life in communion with the Catholic Church.

The unsuccessful attempts to produce even the physical marks of the wound of Christ by natural means, such as hypnotism, help to confirm the verdict of the Belgian doctors.

Attempts at Natural Explanations of the Stigmata

The stigmata being a kind of permanent miracle reminding men of the cruel sufferings of Christ by which their sins were expiated, it is not surprising that they should be an object of particular hatred for the devil and of contradiction for his followers in the world who reject Christ. Atheists regard the stigmata as an aggressive form of miracle challenging their rejection of the supernatural and of the redemption of Christ. They give somewhat the same kind of explanation as they gave of the miracles of Lourdes when they first appeared; hysteria coupled with auto-suggestion or hypnotism. The atheistic Dr. Charcot of the last century, who had a great reputation as a doctor, spent a good deal of time in making experiments in his clinic at Salpetriere in Paris on patients he regarded as hysterical in an endeavor to produce by hypnotism marks on the body resembling the stigmata. Claims were made for partial success during his lifetime, but Dr. Dejerine, who succeeded him, declared that, in the vast number of cases of psychopathics and neuropathics observed by him at the Salpetriere clinic, there was never a single case of bleeding wounds like the stigmata. This is the almost unanimous opinion of doctors of the present day. The explanation of various forms of nervous diseases by means of hysteria belongs to the dark ages of medicine.

While the term "hysteria" was in common use, hardly any two doctors defined it alike. For most doctors and for the public in general, the symptoms of hysteria are abnormal emotionalism, insistent egotism and pathological lying. Dr. Hynek, the famous Prague doctor, who is the author of many books, rightly thinks that the word "hysteria" should be outlawed in civilized society as a most offensive term calculated to destroy a person's moral reputation. In his book on Teresa Neumann, we read the following:

"What really is this disease which renders such immense services to skeptics? In books on medicine it is called the *crux medicorum,* so many are the difficulties encountered in its treatment. In practice, in dealing with confused enigmatical cases where there is nothing upon which a diagnosis may be based, but where the doctor must say something, hysteria is the veritable *Deus ex machina* which saves his reputation. . . .

"Take the treatise on psychiatry of one of the most remarkable professors of our day, Dr. Bleuler. What is our astonishment to find that he has completely demolished the accustomed idea of hysteria. He has not even spared the physical marks of the disease. For him, they no longer exist. In the same way, the very word 'hysteria' is no longer to be found in the records of his clinic at Zurich. The definition of the disease suffers the same fate. According to Bleuler, all that before was negligently classified as 'hysteria', on account of our newer knowledge of psycho-analysis, is nothing else than 'an abnormal form of reaction on exterior life.'"

Fr. Thurston, S.J., agrees with the above in theory, though he finds it hard to get rid of his old habit of using the word "hysteria" in its antiquated sense. In *The Physical Phenomena of Mysticism* (p. 101), he writes:

"What is realized by comparatively few persons outside the medical profession is the fact that a new and, it seems, a much more exact conception of neurosis still commonly called hysteria has come to prevail within the last thirty years, and that these views have been immensely developed and corroborated by the experiences of the Four Years' War. The associations of the word hysteria as it is commonly understood by the public at large, are so misleading and so disparaging to the patient that many neurologists have urged that a new name should be found for it."

Dr. Ewald, the atheistic doctor who carried out the investigation of Teresa Neumann's case along with Dr. Seidl, as already stated, tried to wriggle out of the position in which he found himself and put forward hysteria as an explanation of the phenomena which he admitted to be genuine. However he added: "Many people worthy of the highest esteem have at one time or other shown all the signs of hysteria"!

Dr. de Poray Madeyski, the Polish doctor whose book on Teresa Neumann has been very much quoted by adversaries, after devoting the second half of his book to expounding his own particular view of hysteria, which is a modification of that of Dr. Charcot, concludes:

"The existence of hysteria in the case of Teresa Neumann does not in any way detract from her moral character, from her personal dignity, from her sincerity, from her piety or even from the possibility of her being a real saint; it takes nothing from the merits of her pious intentions nor from those of her virtuous life."

Both these much-quoted doctors, Dr. Ewald and Dr. Madeyski, explicitly admit that Teresa Neumann has none of the symptoms ordinarily associated with hysteria and yet they insist on using the insulting term and, what is worse, Catholic writers quote them without giving the clauses that these men insert to save their own reputations as regards scientific accuracy.

Where Dr. Charcot and other famous doctors failed to produce by natural means anything remotely resembling the physical marks of the stigmata, a Lutheran doctor named Dr. Lechler claims to have succeeded. It should be noticed, however, that he did not know how much to claim, and what he actually claims to have produced, would not, even if it were a fact, be considered for a moment by the Catholic Church as a case of Stigmatization. No witnesses were allowed to be present while Dr. Lechler carried out his experiments, except Lutheran deaconesses; even the name of the subject of the experiment has not been released; it is alleged that it was a girl and she is referred to as Elizabeth K– – –. All traces of marks alleged to have been produced had disappeared before anyone, except the deaconesses, was allowed to see this mysterious Elizabeth K– – –. No further experiment was made on her.

It would be unnecessary to say anything more about the case except for the fact that both Fr. Thurston, S.J., and Fr. Siwek, S.J., take it seriously and refer to it as a case of Stigmatization in a non-Catholic. Fr. Crehen, S.J., in his preface to *Physical Phenomena of Mysticism* by Fr. Thurston, makes the following rather extraordinary statement about this case:

"In 1933 his views (Fr. Thurston's) were very much clarified when a Lutheran doctor in Germany succeeded in producing stigmata by suggestion in an hysterical patient. The circumstances of the occasion were vouched for by reputable physicians . . ."

As already stated, there were no witnesses present except Lutheran deaconesses. A few doctors may have accepted Dr. Lechler's account but that does not get rid of the fact that no doctor was allowed to be present at the experiment.

The following is the account of the case which was published by Dr. Frohlich in 1950, in his book entitled *Konnersreuth To-day*, and his reply to Dr. Lechler:

"In the year 1933 there appeared a book, *Das Rätsel von Konnersreuth im Lichte eines neuen Falles von Stigmatisation,* by Med. Dr. Alfred Lechler, then head of the Elbingerode Institute for Nervous Complaints in the Southern Harz. In this brochure, with 7 photographs, Dr. Lechler asserted that, in the case of the Protestant patient, Elizabeth K– – –, suffering severely from nerve trouble, he had produced 'stigmata' on hands and feet by suggestion and auto-suggestion. We have, however, to consider these 'stigmata' in comparison with previously known woundmarks of stigmatists and in particular with those of Teresa Neumann. We give below a detailed survey, as drawn up by J. M. Hocht in 1938 in the discussion which raged around the case of this 'Protestant stigmatist', from which it is possible quickly to determine the difference between the various kinds of wounds or stigmata as they come into the question in each case. The abovenamed author drew up the following table of comparison.*

* See *Grösse, Erhabenheit und Beurteilung der Stigmatisation. Eine Einführung in die Geschichte der Stigmatisierten.* Waldassen 1939.

Comparative Table of Wounds and Stigmata

(after Höcht)

DR. LECHLER'S PHENOMENA	WOUND MARKS OF STIGMATISTS
ORIGIN: Produced by extraordinary effort of will under the influence of suggestion.	ORIGIN: Spontaneous, without effort of will, in ecstasy during complete suppression of and suggestibility.
ANATOMICAL-PHYSIOLOGICAL CHARACTER	ANATOMICAL-PHYSIOLOGICAL CHARACTER: Deep, gaping wounds, severe bleeding, often daily, in most cases weekly, for years or decades; loss of blood up to a liter. Wounds covered with fine, glassy membrane.
Wounds: quite tiny in extent, mere skin-mutations rather than 'wounds'; only droplike secretions of blood in small, often in tiny quantities.	Further: Wounds penetrating vital tissues (cf. Heart stigmata) which in the ordinary course of nature would involve the death of the sufferer. Wounds not diffusing unpleasant odor. Flow of blood in direction contrary to gravity.
Duration: Wounds vanish after 1-2 days. (at cessation of suggestion.)	*Duration:* Stigmata remain for years and decades, generally against the will of the stigmatist, without inflammation, without discharge, without suppurating and ulcerating.
Associated Factors: Openly exhibited symptoms of hysteria, severe illness.	*Associated Factors:* Above all, no trace of hysteria, on the contrary, a wealth of important mystical phenomena which speak for themselves.

"Extremely important is the note added by Dr. Lechler that the supervision of Elizabeth K– – – was not stringent enough so that he was not able to rule out the possibility of fraudulent manipulation of his medium.

"If, on the basis of the above schedule, we compare Teresa Neumann's woundmarks with the characteristics of genuine stigmata as recorded in the history of Catholic stigmatists, it is seen at once that, in her case, we are dealing with wounds in the sense of those of the classical Catholic stigmatists, while in the case of Elizabeth K– – –, entirely different phenomena are concerned."*

Fr. Poulain, S.J., the well-known authority on mystical theology arrives at the same conclusions as Dr. Fröhlich, as the following quotations from *The Graces of Interior Prayer* show:

"And further, it has been shown (see Imbert, Vol. II, ch. vi, xiv; Surbled, La Morale, Vol. VI, Part II, final chapter; Gombault, L'Imagination, Part IV, ch. ii, pp. 504, 514) that the saints' stigmata presented very great differences from those of the hypnotized persons of whom we have just been speaking.

1. With the first, there are true wounds; the flow of blood is often very abundant. There is nothing similar with the others. There has merely been a swelling or a more or less colored exudation. It is a course imitation only.

2. The first often persists for several years, or reproduce themselves periodically every week. The others are transient.

3. It is not possible to cure the first by means of remedies.

4. The first are often very painful. This fact has not been noted with the others.

---

* From *Kunnersreuth Heute* by Med. Dr. Frölich, pages 75, 76, 77.

5. The first have always been accompanied by ecstasies.

6. Contrary to what is observed in all natural wounds of a certain duration, those of the saints exhibit no fetid odor (sometimes they even emit a perfume), no suppuration, no morbid deterioration of the tissues. And the remarkable thing is that any non-stigmatic wounds from which they may suffer follow the normal course.

"To sum up, if we say that the imagination is capable of producing the stigmatic wounds, we are forced to state it as a fact. without any experimental proof.

"If anyone wishes to prove in a really scientific manner that the imagination, auto-suggestion, that is to say, can produce the stigmata, there is only one way of doing it: instead of proposing mere hypothesis, he must bring similar facts, only of the natural order, that is to say, wounds produced by suggestion, apart from any religious idea. But none have been met with, notwithstanding the extreme good will of doctors and hypnotizers. There is not one example of a real wound produced in a hospital by the excitation of the imagination and the sensibility. Rubefaction, or at the most, reddish sweat have indeed been obtained, although very rarely; but there has never been any flow of blood, and especially no punctures, no tearing of the tissues. And this not even on the soft part of the skin, any more than those occupied by the stigmata of Crucifixion, that is to say, on the inner and very tough surfaces of the hands and feet."

"The essential characters of the stigmata are these: they are wounds, they are localized in the same places as in our Lord's body, they bleed on fixed days, and they cause terrible suffering. The hemorrhage is merely a secondary and intermittent phenomenon. Finally, the wounds make their appearance in places where the skin is thickest and most resistant, on the palms of the hands and the soles of the feet; which never occurs, says Dr. Lefebvre, with morbid hemorrhages." (The Graces of Interior Prayer, Ch. XXXI. Nos. 10 and 11., by Fr. Poulain, S.J.).

Another alleged case of a non-Catholic stigmatist is that of the Hamburg merchant named Monk. Surface wounds appeared on his forehead at intervals of between a month and six weeks and were accompanied by heart attacks. The man practiced no religion and the marks were not in any way associated with the wounds of Christ.*

As neither the case of the elusive Elizabeth K– – – as given by Dr. Lechler, nor that of the Hamburg merchant bears any resemblance to the case of any genuine stigmatist, it is most unfair that Catholic writers should deceive the Catholic public by referring to them as stigmatists.

How Explain the Fact That Most of the Stigmatists Were Women?

It is unquestionably a fact that the number of women who have received the stigmata is many times greater than the number of men. It is understandable that atheistic writers should seize on the fact to discredit this form of miracle, that is confined to the Catholic Church, by representing the stigmata as the effect of emotionalism or hysteria; but one would expect Catholic writers to abstain from acting as propagandists for an atheistic theory now rejected by most doctors. Reasons can be found for the disparity in the numbers without resorting to such theories. The vocation of all true stigmatists is to bear a portion of the physical sufferings of Our Lord and in a mysterious manner to keep Our Blessed

* From *Konnersreuth Heute* by Med. Dr. Fröhlich. pages 77, 78.

Lady company at the foot of the cross. At the actual crucifixion of Our Blessed Lord on Calvary, there were three women present, including Our Blessed Lady and only one man, St. John, the Beloved Disciple. Those writers with the hysteria complex should give reasons for the disproportion in the representation of the sexes on Calvary, before resorting to explanations of the stigmata which are, at the same time, derogatory to the female sex and disrespectful to the Sacred Wounds of Christ which the true stigmata represent. Why should any other explanation be sought than that such is the will of Our Divine Saviour: He has reserved the dignity of the priesthood for men, and given them more frequent opportunities for martyrdom than women; and for the honor of keeping Our Blessed Lady company at the foot of the cross, while not excluding other St. Johns, He has chosen members of the female sex. Women outnumber men in many callings where courage and constancy of a high order are necessary. For instance, women outnumber men in the mission-fields; the number of women in the various religious orders and congregations is far greater than the number of men. Such is the arrangement of Divine Providence.

Besides, resorting to such theories as hysteria to explain the disproportion shows a complete ignorance of what the true stigmata connote. The stigmata are not ornaments, neither are they signs of disease; they are the external signs of participation in the greatest suffering that mortal can be asked to bear, and not for a day or two, but for life. The vocation of the stigmatist demands qualities which are the very opposite of those associated with hysteria in any form; it demands strength of will, heroic courage, deep humility and constancy, not confined to a limited period, but lasting for a lifetime.

Fr. Pio has borne those painful wounds now for forty

years; the sufferings of Teresa Neumann began the year that Fr. Pio received the stigmata, so she, too, has spent forty years of her life in suffering, during thirty-two of which she has borne the stigmata, and she has accompanied Our Blessed Lord in His Passion, from the Agony in the Garden to the Death on the Cross, more than a thousand times. Where, then, in the whole world could one find two other such examples of courage and constancy?

In our own times, when the miraculous character of the stigmata of St. Francis of Assisi was being called into question even by Catholic writers, Divine Providence so arranged that a replica of them should be found, not in Padre Pio of Foggia, but in Teresa Neumann, and a replica of the stigmata of St. Mary Frances of the Five Wounds should be found, not in Teresa Neumann, but in Padre Pio. It is an emphatic refutation of the atheistic explanation of the stigmata and a touching illustration of the meaning of St. Paul's words:

"There is neither Jew nor Greek; there is neither bond nor free; there is neither male nor female. For you are all one in Christ Jesus." (*Galatians* 3:28).

The objection against the miraculous character of the stigmata that, as most of the stigmatists have been women, there is probably some natural explanation such as hysteria has been urged against other extraordinary favors. It has been urged against the devotion to the Sacred Heart of Jesus because the person to whom the revelations concerning it, St. Margaret Mary Alocoque, was a woman, as were St. Gertrude and St. Mechtilde who received revelations about the Sacred Heart before her time. It has been urged also against the Work of Infinite Love because the person to whom the revelations concerning it, Mother Louise Margaret, was a woman.

Fr. Galliffet, S.J., the disciple of Blessed Claude de la Colombiere, who wrote in 1726, gives the following answer to the objection:*

"Those who are opposed to extraordinary graces frequently object that in these matters the testimony of women alone is brought forward, rarely that of men, insinuating thereby that it ought to be mistrusted. It is easy to answer this objection. First, women who are really holy are as much under the influence of the Spirit of God as men; and for this reason alone their testimony is of equal value. Secondly, it is true, as St. Teresa remarks, that the Holy Spirit generally selects the weaker sex for these supernatural graces. His wisdom understands wherefore, but it is on this account that the testimony of women is much more frequent. Thirdly, we must take notice that women who have been highly favored by God, being absolutely under the control of their superiors and directors, were for the most part obliged under obedience to commit to writing all that passed in their inner life, in order that it might be subjected to close examination, God always admirable in His dealings, having thus ordained, in order that the marvels of His love and grace towards souls might be known, and the memory of them preserved in the Church."

Three questions remain to be discussed, two of which are closely connected; the first, are there stigmata of diabolical origin or is it within the power of the devil to produce deep wounds corresponding to the Wounds of Christ, that remain fresh for years: the second, can the stigmata be produced by mystical contemplation alone: the third, what is the connection, if any, between the stigmata and holiness?

---

* *The Adorable Heart of Jesus* by Fr. Galliffet. S. J., Manresa Press, Roehampton, 1897.

Diabolical Stigmata

With regard to the first question, it can be confidently stated that there has been no case within the last hundred years in which the external, physical marks of the stigmata as described in the beginning of this chapter have been produced by natural means such as hypnotism, by diabolical agency, or by a combination of both. It may be presumed that the devil gave such help as he was able to men like Charcot and Lechler whose object was to lessen the esteem of people for the real stigmata. The combined efforts produced nothing more than blisters on the skin that vanished in a day. Herr Mook, referred to above, may well have been one of those on whom the devil tried his experiments.

Has the devil been any more successful in past ages: Cardinal Bona has been quoted as holding the opinion that the devil not only can produce the marks of the stigmata but that he has actually done so. He writes: " . . . The marks of the wounds (of Christ) can be imitated and impressed by the fiend, as so many examples too painfully have proven."*

It is to be noted that all the Cardinal says is that the marks of the wounds "can be imitated and impressed" by the devil; he does not say that the devil can produce deep wounds that remain fresh for years. He adds that there have been many examples of diabolical stigmata, but in none of the examples commonly quoted do we find reference to deep wounds that have remained fresh for years.

The case of diabolical stigmata most commonly referred to, especially by writers who endeavor to disparage the true stigmata, is that of Magdalena de la Cruz, and when referred to, the facts of the case are generally distorted. The

---

* *De dicretione spirituum* Rome 1672. Chapter VII by Cardinal Bona (1609-1674).

following are the facts of the case: Magdalena de la Cruz was born in Spain near Cordoba in 1487. At the age of twelve she was solicited by the devil who appeared to her in human form, and she remained under his power for more than forty years. She entered the Franciscan Convent of Sancta Isabel de los Angeles in 1504, of which convent she afterwards became Abbess. She gained a great reputation for holiness and for thirty-nine years exhibited a series of pseudo-mystical phenomena among which were the stigmata which bled. These she frequently exhibited to people who visited her. In 1543 she fell dangerously ill and confessed that her holiness was only a pretense and that the extraordinary phenomena in her life were the work of the devil. When she repented, all these phenomena, including the stigmata, ceased and never reappeared. She passed the last seventeen years of her life in the convent of Sancta Clara, deeply penitent, and died in 1560. With regard to her stigmata, it is not stated that they were deep wounds or that they were permanent. As she was fond of displaying them, it may be presumed that they were produced by the devil for each occasion, and that they disappeared during the intervals. At all events they disappeared in 1643 when she repented and never reappeared. Hers is the most extreme case and most commonly quoted of the devil's attempts to deceive people by counterfeiting the stigmata, and it is to be noted that Divine Providence did not allow the deception to be permanent. Much the same may be said about all other cases of stigmata "imitated and impressed" by the devil.*

* See *The Physical Phenomena of Mysticism* by Montague Summers, New York, 1950.

Can the Stigmata Be the Result of Mystical Contemplation?

The theory that the stigmata can be the result of mystical contemplation is of recent origin; the late Dom Alois Mager, O.S.B., of Salzburg is its chief exponent. As Dorn Mager holds that the stigmata can be prodzuced naturally by hypnosis or suggestion on hysterical subjects, it must be presumed that he is using the word "stigmata" in its medical sense of surface wounds or blisters. At the time that he and Fr. Thurston were writing there was confusion not only about the meaning of the word "stigmata" but about the physical characteristics of the stigmata of the historic stigmatists, even of those of St. Francis of Assisi. That confusion has been dispelled in a providential way by the appearance of the stigmata on the members of Padre Pio and Teresa Neumann. Dom Mager had an opportunity of testing his theory by an investigation of the cases of either Padre Pio and Teresa Neumann. He paid two visits of an hour each to Konnersreuth and would go no more; he never visited Padre Pio. He cannot, therefore, be regarded as an authority on the subject. There are several objections against this theory, the two most serious of which are: first, that if mystical contemplation or a very high degree of sanctity could produce the stigmata, all the canonized saints should have had them, and second, that it. does not leave room for the use of free will in the stigmatists.

While most of the stigmatists led edifying lives and persevered to the end, a few fell away. Among those who fell away there were some like Marie-Julie Jahenny whose stigmata differed from anything ever produced by hypnotism or suggestion and appear to have been genuine. If we accept the traditional opinion of the Church that the stigmata are gifts of God, which like other special gifts of God, demand the free co-operation of the recipient and give no guarantee of perseverance to the end, there is no difficulty in explaining the case of Marie-Julie Jahenny.

The third question, namely, whether there is any connection between charisms such as the stigmata (assuming that the stigmata are charisms) has been discussed in a learned article in the July 1953 issue of *The Irish Theological Quarterly* by Fr. E. McMullin. As his conclusions are the same as those to be drawn from what has been said in the present chapter we give them here:

"There are two possible methods of approach. The one we prefer is to suppose that preternatural phenomena in the lives of the saints are charisms of a sort: they are given for the edification of others, and not at all to aid the person's own spiritual life. But they are not completely unrelated to sanctity, because we observe that they are far more frequent latterly in the lives of saints than in those of other people: 'although the grace of miracles is, and may be, conferred on sinners, generally however it is conferred only on the just and holy'. We might argue, for instance, that the best sort of apologetic sign is not merely a miracle, but a miracle done by a saint, since attention is drawn not merely to God, but also to the way in which one must reach Him. However, theoretical reasonings like this are of little value, since they did not apparently govern the distribution of charisms in the primitive Church, and in any case, God's ways are not ours. What is important now, as it was in Patristic times, is the observed fact; the theology of charisms originated from the observation of certain facts rather than from theory, so that it is only reasonable that it should be modified as new facts may warrant. 'We observe that charisms nowadays are usually associated with saints, and deduce a certain probability (no more) that a person who is blessed with these powers, is also a saint'. The Fathers observed that charisms in their time were not usually associated with saints, and so made no such deduction, and, in fact, warmly attacked the Donatists for linking the two. An historical change in the distribution of charisms seems to be indicated, if these observations are accurate. There is no reason against such a change, and indeed, one would not have to search very far for some excellent reasons in its favor."